IRON! FOODS THAT GIVE YOU DAILY IRON

Healthy Eating for Kids

Children's Diet & Nutrition Books

All Rights reserved. No part of this book may be reproduced or used in any way or form or by any means whether electronic or mechanical, this means that you cannot record or photocopy any material ideas or tips that are provided in this book.

Copyright 2016

What is iron for?

Iron is an important mineral that our body needs. It is needed to transport oxygen to all body parts.

Here are some of the high iron foods.

Spinach

Its bright and vibrant looking leaves are nourishing. Spinach leaves that look fully alive have a greater concentration of Vitamin C. Spinach contains health-supportive nutrients known as glycoglycerolipids.

Swiss Chard

Swiss chard leaves have 13 different polyphenol antioxidants. Chard also contains phytonutrients called betalains.

Swiss chard is one of the most nutritious vegetables ever known. It is a popular vegetable around the Mediterranean. It ranked second to spinach.

Parsley

Its primary role is a garnish on other foods. But this vegetable has a delicious and vibrant taste. Aside from that, parsley also has wonderful healing properties. This is the world's most popular herb and is highly nutritious.

Red meat

It is an excellent source of iron. It provides heme iron. A serving of beef contains 2.5 milligrams of iron. Organ meats such as liver or beef heart contain more iron.

Red meat in your meals helps ensure your iron daily recommended level is achieved. Animal-based foods are part of your diet.

Chicken or poultry

Chicken liver can give us iron. Chicken hearts and giblets are also good sources of iron.

Fish and Seafood

These are rich sources of iron. Oysters, fish and clams can provide us with high amounts of heme iron. One can get 4.5 mg of iron per serving of oysters.

Beans and Green Leafy Vegetables

These are good sources of iron. They are even better than meat in volume, but only provide non-heme iron. Eating foods containing iron will increase iron absorption in the body. Vegetable eaters don't easily acquire iron deficiency.

Broccoli and Cauliflower

These plant-based foods contain non-heme iron and it is limited in what the body can do with it.

Raisins

These are one of the nutritious dried fruits. Raisins contain large amount of iron. These can be added to your sweet treats. Yogurt and oatmeal can taste better when you add these dried fruits.

Brussels Sprouts

These tasty veggies are very healthy and are excellent source of iron. These are good sources of antioxidants. They can also give you vitamins, folates and fiber.

Lentils

Lentils are good sources of iron and protein. Vitamins and nutrients are contained in these colorful legumes. These veggies can also provide us with essential amino acids. These are used to spice up soups, pastas, stews and many other dishes. sews and many others.

Pumpkin Seeds

One milligram of iron is contained in a handful of pumpkin seeds. Pumpkin seeds are its best when eaten raw.

Soybeans

This super food contains protein, good fat, fiber, iron and other minerals. For a healthy and delicious meal, soybeans are added to soups or chili.

Arugula

These are dark greens. These have countless health benefits. Arugula is known for its rich iron content. These can improve the health of your red blood cells. These are best enjoyed as green leafy salad.

Pinto Beans

These colored beans can give you essential vitamins and minerals. Just a cup of boiled pinto beans can give you the recommended value of these vitamins including iron.

Whole Wheat Pasta

This should be a part of your healthy, balanced diet. Eating this will provide you with magnesium, calcium, potassium and iron.

Brown Rice

It is a versatile food on Earth. It is known as an important health food. It is highly rich in fiber that helps get rid of toxins. Its high iron content can also fight anemia and fatigue. It can give us iron-rich meal.

Black Beans

They contain fiber, protein and iron. They are energy boosters. A one cup serving of black beans can give you 20% of the recommended daily intake of iron.

Oatmeal

Adding oatmeal to your diet can greatly reduce iron deficiency. It is considered as a fantastic health food. This is an easy breakfast food.

Prune Juice

This is a potent source of iron. It is also tasty and delicious. It is also high in Vitamin C that lets your body easily absorb iron. So, why not have a glass of it?

Potatoes

These are versatile foods. Vegetarians love this food as it is iron-rich. Potatoes are also packed with Vitamin C.

Tofu

It is a nutritious food known around the world. It is highly rich in iron and other minerals. Its bland taste is made tastier with sauces and seasonings.

Strawberries

These fruits are a good source of iron. These are used as side dish especially with breakfast. Strawberries are also rich in vitamin C.

People worry about how to get enough iron in their diet. We know that meat is traditionally known as the main sources of iron.

That is why vegetarians thought of different iron sources. Several vegetables can give us the recommended amount of iron every day.